T0400761

Life Cycles

A Dog's Life Cycle

by Jamie Rice

Ideas for Parents and Teachers

Bullfrog Books let children practice reading informational text at the earliest reading levels. Repetition, familiar words, and photo labels support early readers.

Before Reading

- Discuss the cover photo. What does it tell them?
- Look at the picture glossary together. Read and discuss the words.

Read the Book

- "Walk" through the book and look at the photos. Let the child ask questions. Point out the photo labels.
- Read the book to the child, or have him or her read independently.

After Reading

- Prompt the child to think more. Ask: Puppies are born in litters. What other animals are born in groups?

Bullfrog Books are published by Jump!
5357 Penn Avenue South
Minneapolis, MN 55419
www.jumplibrary.com

Library of Congress Cataloging-in-Publication Data

Names: Rice, Jamie, author.
Title: A dog's life cycle / by Jamie Rice.
Description: Bullfrog books. | Minneapolis, MN: Jump!, Inc., [2023] | Series: Life cycles
Includes index. | Audience: Ages 5–8
Identifiers: LCCN 2021048365 (print)
LCCN 2021048366 (ebook)
ISBN 9781636908281 (hardcover)
ISBN 9781636908298 (paperback)
ISBN 9781636908304 (ebook)
Subjects: LCSH: Dogs—Life cycles
Juvenile literature.
Classification: LCC SF426.5 .R526 2023 (print)
LCC SF426.5 (ebook)
DDC 636.7—dc23/eng/20211004
LC record available at
https://lccn.loc.gov/2021048365
LC ebook record available at
https://lccn.loc.gov/2021048366

Editor: Eliza Leahy
Designer: Emma Bersie

Photo Credits: cynoclub/Shutterstock, cover; ARTSILENSE/Shutterstock, 1; Liliya Kulianionak/Shutterstock, 3; Anke Van Wyk/Dreamstime, 4, 5; Serhii Akhtemiichuk/Dreamstime, 6–7, 23tr; Sandra Huber/Shutterstock, 8; Anna Hoychuk/Shutterstock, 9, 23bl; LeventeGyori/Shutterstock, 10–11; Marina Olena/Shutterstock, 12–13, 23br; Sigma _ S/Shutterstock, 14, 22l; Rita _ Kochmarjova/Shutterstock, 15; Tierfotoagentur/Alamy, 16–17; SvetikovaV/Shutterstock, 18–19, 23tl; otsphoto/Shutterstock, 20–21; Ermolaev Alexander/Shutterstock, 22r; Gelpi/Shutterstock, 24.

Printed in the United States of America at Corporate Graphics in North Mankato, Minnesota.

Table of Contents

Eat, Sleep, Play

This dog is going to have puppies!

Puppies grow inside her.

She carries them for 63 days!

Puppies are born!

The group is called a litter.

litter

Puppies are tiny.
They can't hear.
Their eyes are closed.

They drink Mom's milk.

Puppies sleep.

They grow.

Their eyes open.

They can hear.

They start to walk.

They run and play!

dog
food

They eat a lot.

They grow big.
This dog turns one!
Now it is an adult.

HAPP
BIRTHD

Dogs have puppies of their own.

Life Cycle of a Dog

A dog's life cycle has just two stages. Take a look!

Picture Glossary

adult
A fully grown dog.

litter
A group of baby animals that are born at the same time to the same mother.

milk
The white fluid produced by female animals to feed their young.

puppies
Dogs that are not fully grown.

Index

To Learn More

Finding more information is as easy as 1, 2, 3.

1. Go to www.factsurfer.com
2. Enter "adog'slifecycle" into the search box.
3. Choose your book to see a list of websites.